For Ren, Emma, Bella, and young readers everywhere...
May Lisa's story inspire you to follow your dreams.
—MG

I would like to dedicate this to my nieces, Alice, Sofia, and Arianna,
to always follow their truest dreams.
—SP

ACKNOWLEDGMENTS

Heartfelt thanks to Jackie Maduff and Larry Kirshbaum, without
whom this book would never have happened.

Thank you to Christine Burrill and Lee Cohen.
Special thanks to Emil Sher for his exquisite adaptation.

Deepest appreciation to my wonderful editor, Samantha Gentry, and the
Little, Brown family for their amazing belief and support of this book.

Hugs for Bentley.

Enormous gratitude to Sonia Possentini for her extraordinary artistry.

Finally, to the memory of my beloved sister, Renée,
and to her children—Michele, Sarah, Jonathan, and Rachel—who
inspire me every day to go out in the world and share the
precious message of their grandmother.

Hold On to Your Music

*The Inspiring True Story
of the Children of Willesden Lane*

By Mona Golabek and Lee Cohen

Adapted by Emil Sher
Illustrated by Sonia Possentini

LITTLE, BROWN AND COMPANY
New York Boston

Snow-covered palaces sparkled as Lisa rode the
trolley through the streets of Vienna toward her piano
lesson. As she passed the symphony hall, she dreamed
of the day when she would perform on a grand stage
and play the music of Mozart and Beethoven.

Every week, when Lisa arrived at her piano teacher's studio, she found him sitting in the same worn armchair.

But today he stood outside the door.

"I'm afraid there are no more lessons." His voice was slowed by sadness. "There are new laws that won't allow me to teach Jewish children."

Lisa didn't understand.

"I'm so sorry, Lisa. But it's best that you ask your parents to explain."

When Lisa arrived home, she was heartbroken.

She told her parents what her piano teacher had said.

"Many families like ours are going through painful times," her father said. "We've been made to feel that being Jewish is a crime."

Lisa thought of the friends and parents she saw at synagogue every week. They had done nothing wrong, and neither had she.

"Why should I have to stop taking lessons? It's not fair!"

Lisa's father gently brushed her cheek.

"It hurts to be told you can't do the things you love just because others' hearts are filled with hate," he said. "But that doesn't mean you have to stop playing."

Lisa's mother held out her hand and led her to the piano.

"Whatever tomorrow brings, Liseleh, you must always remember to hold on to your music. It will be your best friend."

Together, they played a duet, carried away by the melody, leaving their worries behind.

Lisa practiced the piano with her mother every day.

As the snow continued to fall, there was talk of war in the air.

"Vienna will not be safe for a young child," her father said softly.

"Where will we go?"

Her mother cradled Lisa's face in her hands.

"Not us, Liseleh. Just you."

They described the special trains that would take children just like her to Britain, where she would be safe and could follow her dream.

"Aren't you coming with me?"

Her father shook his head as Lisa's mother hugged her tightly.

Lisa was frightened.

She worried she wasn't brave enough to go by herself.

On her last morning in Vienna, Lisa slowly walked through her apartment.

She whispered goodbye to her piano.

She looked at family photographs until she could remember them with her eyes closed.

She wondered when she would sleep in her bed again.

The train station was filled with a symphony of sobs.

Children with numbers strung around their neck clung to their parents.

Lisa could see her papa struggling not to cry.

"Remember to—" her mother started to say through her tears.

"I won't forget, Mama. I'll hold on to my music and never let go."

On the train, Lisa felt very alone.
She wished the train would come to a screeching halt,
but it kept rolling farther from home.

All day and all night, Lisa heard the clickety-clack of the wheels
as young children called out for their parents in their sleep.
Lisa gazed through the window, pretending to play for the
moonlit windmills. As she imagined the music, she felt less alone.

After a long journey, they finally reached London.
Lisa stood in a sea of anxious Jewish children waiting to
be taken to their new homes.

"Number 158!" boomed a woman with a wide smile, double-checking her list.
Lisa clutched her suitcase and raised her hand.
"You're off to Willesden Lane, dear."

"Welcome, dearest. I'm Mrs. Cohen, the head of the home." She led Lisa toward a brick house where dozens of children waited to greet her. When Lisa saw the beautiful lilac garden, she was hopeful about her new life.

By the time dinner was served, Lisa had learned all the house rules and made a new friend.

Gina told her there were thirty-two boys and girls living at Willesden Lane who had also left their families behind.

But no one had told Lisa about the old piano tucked away in a corner of the house.

She had just begun to touch the keys when Mrs. Cohen walked up.

"I've been waiting for a child who knows how to play the piano! Might that be you?"

Lisa hugged Mrs. Cohen with all her might.

"I'm guessing that's a yes."

During the day, Lisa worked at a factory sewing uniforms for soldiers.
In the evening, her fingers danced along the piano keys, filling the
house with joy.

But one afternoon, the piano was gone. Mrs. Cohen walked in and saw Lisa about to cry.

"I had to move it to the basement, where it's safer. Mrs. Cohen's lips were pinched with worry. "Britain is at war. Bombs will soon be falling from the sky."

At night, as the bombs dropped onto London, Lisa practiced in the basement.

The closer the bombs, the louder she played.

The sound of the explosions faded as Lisa's music soared.

Each night, Mrs. Cohen listened to Lisa play the piano.
"I see how much the music means to you. Perhaps you should study at the Royal Academy of Music. It is one of our best schools," she explained.

"Would they ever accept me?" Lisa asked. "I'm a Jewish refugee."
"You're also a very gifted pianist," Mrs. Cohen said.
"But I don't have a teacher to help me prepare."
Mrs. Cohen beamed.
"Don't worry, dear. Your friends will help you."
   Each night, the children of Willesden Lane helped Lisa with everything from her scales to her posture until the day of her audition arrived.

Gina held Lisa's hand as they walked
into the academy.

She didn't let go until Lisa's name
was called.

Lisa stepped into a recital room and
took her place at the piano.

Three judges listened as her music swirled and floated around them.
Lisa hoped they were pleased with her performance.
"They said I'll know soon," she told Gina on the way home.

Each day felt like forever while she waited.

Two weeks later, Mrs. Cohen handed Lisa an envelope.

She was too nervous to read it, so Gina tore it open.

"You've been accepted!" she shouted.

The children erupted in cheers.

Mrs. Cohen wiped the tears from her eyes.

———— ◆ ————

On her first morning at the academy, Lisa imagined her parents walking her to the front door, bursting with pride.

She remembered her very first piano lesson as a young girl back in Vienna, her small hands barely reaching the keys.

Now she was much closer to her dream of performing on a grand stage.

Then came the news everyone was waiting for—the war was over!

After years of waiting for peace, everyone was hungry for celebrations.

It was time for Lisa's debut!

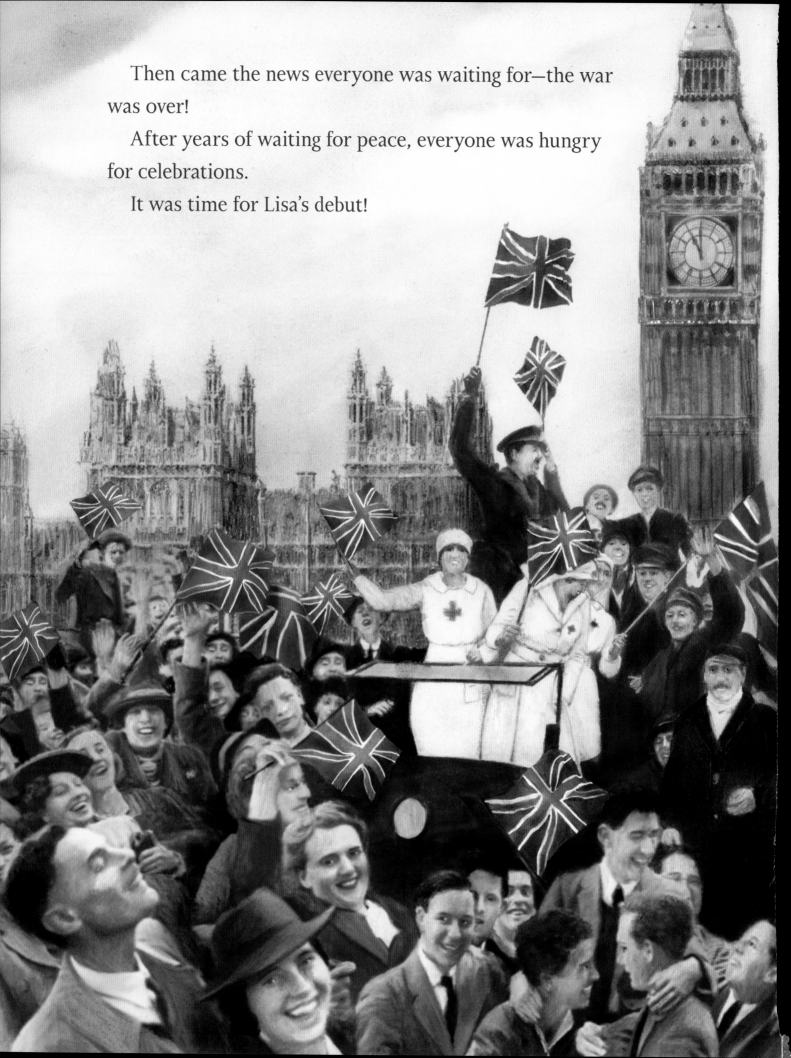

Mrs. Cohen and the children of Willesden Lane filled the front rows of a packed concert hall.

All eyes were on Lisa, who sat perfectly still at a grand piano.

She took a deep breath, pictured her mother by her side, and began to play.

The audience was up on its feet,
cheering the moment the concert came
to an end.

"I kept my promise, Mama," Lisa
said softly, taking a bow. "I held on to
my music and never let go."

Dear Reader,

As a concert pianist and storyteller, I have shared the story of my mother, Lisa Jura, with countless people through my one-woman show, *The Pianist of Willesden Lane*, and my book, *The Children of Willesden Lane*. Her story showcases the power of music and how one teenage refugee held on to her dreams, survived the Holocaust, and ultimately became a beacon of hope for all her peers.

When I was a little girl, my mother taught me and my sister, Renée, to play the piano. I remember our lessons always being magical. She would tell us about her life as a young Jewish girl, who dreamed of becoming an accomplished concert pianist, living in pre–World War II Vienna. We learned about great composers, like Beethoven and Mozart, and she would remind us that "each piece of music tells a story."

Lisa never forgot what her mother told her on that cold winter day very long ago in Vienna: "*Hold on to your music. It will be your best friend.*" It was that phrase that guided Lisa through this dark period in her life. Music gave her the strength to face hard times and an uncertain future, and it provided courage for the other refugee children she lived with on Willesden Lane. The music reminded them of what they had left behind and what they had lost.

Just like for my mother, music has also given me hope and courage. This compelling tribute has already moved hundreds of thousands of students and adults across the globe, but I know that now, in a time when so much is uncertain, I need to share this story with an even younger audience to encourage the importance of standing up against bigotry and hatred. I wrote *Hold On to Your Music* because I wanted to inspire young readers to think about what they hold dear when facing difficult times.

I hope my mother's story will guide you to find your own courage and fill your heart with the magic to follow your dream.

Your friend always,

Mona Golabek

Mona, Lisa, and Renée.

HISTORICAL BACKGROUND

Vienna, the capital of Austria, was not only home to Lisa and her family but also to many Jewish people, whose contributions helped make it a bustling, wonderful place to live.

But in 1938, life for Viennese Jews changed when Nazi Germany took control of Austria. Adolf Hitler, the leader of the Nazis, hated Jews and didn't believe they should be treated the same way as others. He didn't believe they belonged because they practiced a different religion and had different traditions and beliefs. He blamed them for Germany's defeat in World War I, and he compared them to a disease that had to be stopped before it spread.

The Nazis created laws in Austria that made it very difficult for Jews to take part in daily life. They were fired from their jobs. They were banned from most public parks. They were kicked out of their homes. Jewish children were forced to leave their classmates and go to separate schools. And young musicians like Lisa were told they had to stop taking lessons.

A difficult life for Jews was made much worse after the nights of November 9 and 10, 1938. Mobs of citizens and Nazi police destroyed Jewish businesses and set synagogues on fire in Austria and Germany when word spread that a Jewish man had killed a Nazi official. These attacks became known as Kristallnacht, the "Night of Broken Glass." Some Jews were killed, and many were imprisoned.

Not everyone stood by and watched as Jews continued to live in fear. After Kristallnacht, a group of Jews and Christians believed children would be safest if they were beyond Hitler's reach. A plan was hatched to take children by train across Europe to the safety of Britain. The first Kindertransport—or "children's transport"—arrived in England on December 2, 1938. The last one left Germany on September 1, 1939, just hours before World War II began.

Over 10,000 children—about 7,500 of whom were Jewish—had been saved because of the Kindertransport. Like Lisa, they left their loved ones behind, and many were the only survivors in their families. The Second World War took the lives of six million Jews—including 1.5 million children. Their deaths were part of what has become known as the Holocaust.

For more information on the educational initiative around this story from the Koret Foundation and USC Shoah Foundation, visit IWitness.USC.edu/willesdenlane.

Lisa Jura, age 16.

Mrs. Cohen and the children of Willesden Lane.

Lisa Jura and the children of Willesden Lane.

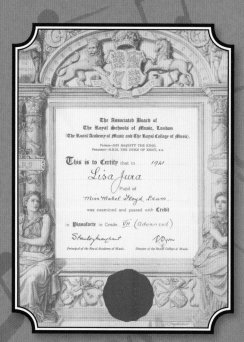

Lisa's certificate from the Royal Academy of Music.

Lisa at the piano, age 21.